FLORA

Birthday Book

This book belongs to

. . . .

FLORA

Birthday Book

January

1 _____

_____

Echinacea purpurea
'Magnus'

2 _____

_____

3 _____

_____

4 _____

_____

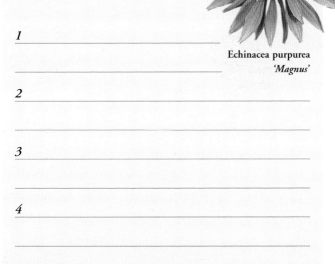

Opposite page: Salvia × sylvestris *'Mainacht'*

January

5
_____

_____

6
_____

_____

7
_____

_____

8
_____

_____

9
_____

_____

10
_____

_____

11
_____

_____

Opposite page: Tulipa, *Triumph Group,* *'Kees Nelis'*

January

12

13

14

15

16

17

18

January

19

20

21

22

23

24

25

Adenium obesum

26 _____

_____

27 _____

_____

28 _____

_____

29 _____

_____

30 _____

_____

31 _____

_____

Opposite page: Leucospermum cordifolium

February

1 _____

_____

Camellia japonica
'Anita'

2 _____

_____

3 _____

_____

4 _____

_____

Opposite page: Fuchsia *'Brutus'*

February

5

6

7

8

9

10

11

12

13

14

15

16

17

18

Moraea villosa

February

19 _____

_____

20 _____

_____

21 _____

_____

22 _____

_____

23 _____

_____

24 _____

_____

25 _____

_____

Zinnia *'Coral Beauty'*

February

26 _____

_____

27 _____

_____

28 _____

_____

29 _____

_____

March

1 _____

_____

Rosa, *Modern, Modern
Shrub, 'James Galway'*

2 _____

_____

3 _____

_____

4 _____

_____

Opposite page: Dioon spinulosum

5 _____

_____

6 _____

_____

7 _____

_____

8 _____

_____

9 _____

_____

10 _____

_____

11 _____

_____

Opposite page: Gloriosa rothschildiana

March

12

13

14

15

16

17

18

19

20

21

22

23

24

25

Rosa, *Modern, Cluster-flowered (Floribunda), 'English Sonnet'*

March

26
_____

_____

27
_____

_____

28
_____

_____

29
_____

_____

30
_____

_____

31
_____

_____

☙

Opposite page: Rhododendron *cultivar*

April

❧

Scabiosa caucasica
'Alba'

1 _____

_____

2 _____

_____

3 _____

_____

4 _____

_____

Opposite page: Lupinus *'Bishop's Tipple'*

April

5

6

7

8

9

10

11

Paphiopedilum haynaldianum

12

13

14

15

16

17

18

April

19
_____

_____

20
_____

_____

21
_____

_____

22
_____

_____

23
_____

_____

24
_____

_____

25
_____

_____

Opposite page: Erigeron peregrinus, *in the wild, in Colorado, USA*

April

26

_____

_____

27

_____

_____

28

_____

_____

29

_____

_____

30

_____

_____

May

&

Camellia *'Night Rider'*

1 _____

_____

2 _____

_____

3 _____

_____

4 _____

_____

May

5 _____

_____

6 _____

_____

7 _____

_____

8 _____

_____

9 _____

_____

10 _____

_____

11 _____

_____

12

13

14

15

16

17

18

Opposite page: Cyclamen persicum

May

19 _____

_____

20 _____

_____

21 _____

_____

22 _____

_____

23 _____

_____

24 _____

_____

25 _____

_____

Rosa, *Modern, Modern Shrub, 'Anna Zinkeisen'*

May

26 _____

_____

27 _____

_____

28 _____

_____

29 _____

_____

30 _____

_____

31 _____

_____

June

Rosa, *Modern, Large-flowered (Hybrid Tea),* 'Blue Nile'

1

2

3

4

Opposite page: Quercus texana

June

5
_____

_____

6
_____

_____

7
_____

_____

8
_____

_____

9
_____

_____

10
_____

_____

11
_____

_____

Opposite page: Protea aristata

June

12

13

14

15

16

17

18

Nelumbo *'Carolina Queen'*

19 _____

_____

20 _____

_____

21 _____

_____

22 _____

_____

23 _____

_____

24 _____

_____

25 _____

_____

June

26

27

28

29

30

Opposite page: Dracaena reflexa *'Song of India'*

July

&

1 _____

_____

Muscari armeniacum
'Cantab'

2 _____

_____

3 _____

_____

4 _____

_____

Opposite page: Iris, *Tall Bearded,* *'Lord Baltimore'*

July

5

6

7

8

9

10

11

July

12

13

14

15

16

17

18

Opposite page: Rosa, *Cluster-flowered (Floribunda), 'Violet Carson'*

July

19

20

21

22

23

24

25

Primula vialii

26

27

28

29

30

31

August

Tigridia pavonia

1 _____
_____

2 _____

3 _____

4 _____
_____

Opposite page: Waterfalls make attractive garden features

August

5 _____

_____

6 _____

_____

7 _____

_____

8 _____

_____

9 _____

_____

10 _____

_____

11 _____

_____

Opposite page: Fuchsia *'Ruth'*

August

12
_____

_____

13
_____

_____

14
_____

_____

15
_____

_____

16
_____

_____

17
_____

_____

18
_____

_____

August

19

20

21

22

23

24

25

Papaver rupifragum

August

26

_____

27

_____

28

_____

29

_____

30

_____

31

_____

Opposite page: Eucalyptus pauciflora, *in the wild, Australia*

September

1 _____

Nymphaea caerulea
'Colorata'

_____

2 _____

_____

3 _____

_____

4 _____

_____

September

5

6

7

8

9

10

11

September

12

13

14

15

16

17

18

Opposite page: Vriesea *'Mariae'*

September

19

20

21

22

23

24

25

Iris *'Purple Rain'*

26
_____

_____

27
_____

_____

28
_____

_____

29
_____

_____

30
_____

_____

October

❧

1
_____

_____

Telopea speciosissima
cultivar

2
_____

_____

3
_____

_____

4
_____

_____

Opposite page: Chamaecyparis lawsoniana *cultivar*

October

5

6

7

8

9

10

11

Opposite page: **Tulipa**, *Single Late Group*, *'Bleu Aimable'*

October

12

13

14

15

16

17

18

October

19

20

21

22

23

24

25

Tulipa, *Greigii Group, 'Yellow Dawn'*

26

_____

_____

27

_____

_____

28

_____

_____

29

_____

_____

30

_____

_____

31

_____

_____

Opposite page: × **Potinara** *Afternoon Delight* '*Magnificent*'

November

Nymphaea *cultivar*

1 _____

_____

2 _____

_____

3 _____

_____

4 _____

_____

Opposite page: Richea pandanifolia, *in the wild, in Tasmania, Australia*

November

5

6

7

8

9

10

11

Opposite page: Rhododendron, *Deciduous Azalea,* 'Rêve d'Amour'

November

12

13

14

15

16

17

18

November

19

20

21

22

23

24

25

Plumeria rubra *'Rosy Dawn'*

November

26 _____

_____

27 _____

_____

28 _____

_____

29 _____

_____

30 _____

_____

Opposite page: Sempervivum *'Hall's Hybrid'*

December

Zinnia *'Oklahoma Salmon'*

1 _____

_____

2 _____

_____

3 _____

_____

4 _____

_____

Opposite page: Gladiolus callianthus

December

5

6

7

8

9

10

11

Echinacea purpurea *'White Swan'*

12

13

14

15

16

17

18

December

19

20

21

22

23

24

25

Tagetes patula *'Jolly Jester'*

December

26

_____

_____

27

_____

_____

28

_____

_____

29

_____

_____

30

_____

_____

31

_____

_____

Notes

. . . .

. . . .

. . . .

. . . .

. . . .

. . . .

. . . .

. . . .

. . . .

. . . .

. . . .

. . . .

. . . .

. . . .

. . . .

. . . .

. . . .

Opposite page: **Rosa**, *Modern, Modern Shrub*, 'Tess of the d'Urbervilles'

Notes

Notes

....
....
....
....
....
....
....
....
....
....
....
....
....
....
....
....
....
....

Published by Timber Press Inc.
133 SW 2nd Avenue, Suite 450, Portland,
OR 97204-3527 U.S.A.
503-227-2878 (telephone) 503-227-3070 (fax)

http://www.timberpress.com

Produced by Global Book Publishing Pty. Ltd.
1/181 High Street, Willoughby NSW 2068, Australia
Ph +61 2 9967 3100 Fax +61 2 9967 5891
Email rightsmanager@globalpub.com.au

ISBN 0 88192 609 4

Printed In Hong Kong by Sing Cheong Printing Company
Film separation by Pica Digital Pte Ltd, Singapore